'*Lyrebird* slowly circles its heartbreak through understatement, poetic revelation, imagistic accord. It admits to its shortcomings gracefully, knows there is no way to write what cannot be undone.'

— Jenny Boully, author of *Betwixt-and-Between*

'Loose with ghosts, absences, light, shadow, memory, time, and dreamwork, *Lyrebird*'s moving song is perforated with echoes and shards of our beautiful earth, our lost secrets, and the things for which we long and of which we let go.'

— Jennifer S. Cheng, author of *Moon*

'*Lyrebird* conjures life from absence, and part of that conjuring means attending to the world around and beyond us, so we might find "ways to occupy the spaces between worlds." Meredith Clark has written a glowing portal that calls us through to wherever we need to go.'

— Steven Dunn, author of *water & power*

Lyrebird. Meredith Clark

PLATYPUS PRESS, ENGLAND

ISBN 978-1-913007-08-9

First Edition, 2020

10 9 8 7 6 5 4 3 2 1

Book and cover design by Peter Barnfather
Cover art by Fred Ingrams
 Sunset on Anchor Drove, July 2018
 Acrylic on board
 61 × 61 cm
 fredingrams.com
Typeset in Bergamo Pro, FontSite Inc.
Printed and bound by Clays Ltd, Elcograf S.p.A.

Published by Platypus Press

For you, from the beginning.

Lyrebird.

One

In the days before I knew whether or not you were real, I started writing to you, speaking to the chance of you in my mind, unclear whether the words were an invitation. They were an introduction just the same.

We traveled that weekend to an island where the woods were dark as memory, and I wore a pair of simple black boots I'd had since I was twelve. Milk fog as the wind went by. A picture of us at the top of a mountain. A first photo of you, or simply a photo of the two of us and the thin air. I did not know if the thought of you framed a presence or a vanishing.

What if, before you were born, your parents had taken a picture of themselves on a mountaintop, where the wind took a piece of your mother's hair and blew it across to touch your father like a tentacle with its own will? Would some part of you forever carry a wildness, a little wind, your doors loose on hinges where the gale goes through?

What is the first part of the song you sing?

Your father ran back to the car for warmth, but I stood a moment longer. A signal tower above the valley; I was catching signals for you, I was tuning them in.

Am I writing you into being?

I dream that I am moving out of an apartment. Your father and his family are moving too. We are to leave the place filled and cannot carry anything with us.

I put on a record as we enter the bright hall. The last thing I think before the door closes is how beautiful the music sounds in that room. It hits so cleanly on the hardwood floors.

The dark now is an early dark, and it lasts.

Coming home this evening, a small child stood in a dimly lit yard. Hat on. Beaming. "Thank you for waiting," her father called. He came down the steps to take her hand. This is a moment she will never remember. She is too small, and it is not important.

Already, I am writing to you. We are not even sure of your place in the world, but my body is changed, and so.

If each moment from now on is shared, then these are your things too. There is so much telling to do.

Dream that in a parking lot in Tokyo, an amusement park has been erected. In the footprint of a parking space, a free-fall ride takes passengers on a trip that lodges their stomachs into their ribcages for a moment. I experience it myself, the seconds stretching exponentially until I hit the ground safely.

I ask another rider for her thoughts. "The thrill," she explains, "is a displaced thrill. It has nothing to do with the fall. When you are about to drop, you recognize, quite longingly, the thrill of returning home."

A video of a naturalist, speaking of lyrebirds. Footage

shows the bird singing his song, which is actually a piecework of all the sounds in the forest. Other birds, a chainsaw, a camera shutter. In this way, he attracts a mate. He preserves her immediate history. He sings her world back to her.

B says she called the ghost to her. Practically a taunt in the cemetery. "If you're out there," she said, "then come on. I'm ready."

Later, the cowboy appeared at the foot of her bed like a thin-air projection, gesturing wildly. He shook his head and waved his arms as though telling someone far off not to walk through a door.

"Wake up," she told the man sleeping next to her. "Do you see him?" He did not.

The last few years, there have been several invitations.

Beneath the river, there is one pale stone. Clear as a destination.

Bled today.

You are no less real for being less imminent.

These are the pictures of us from the time you were

here: A photo of your father, very clever, with my underwear as his pocket square. A photo with Canada behind us. And here is the place where the picture was taken in someone's pocket—seen here on my telephone, the dark becomes a mirror.

The clairvoyant knew.

"Pregnant," she said.

Impossible, I thought, until I started encountering scents so powerfully it was like walking into a wall.

"Here, you can see," the nurse said, shifting the monitor. "You are so early along that all we can make out is this little cluster of cells." A planet, viewed from afar. It was the last I saw of you.

On my wall, I've tacked a map of the Yukon, courtesy of the department of the interior, 1898. For miles and miles above the 62nd parallel, there is only the clean paper of the map itself, with the marking: UNEXPLORED. Later, a dotted line reading: *Supposed course of Macmillan River*.

Draw a map of loss. What were the possibilities? What is the scale?

If we have all chosen to be here, what makes us miserable is that the memory is gone.

The green wall. The red door screaming, *This is an opening*.

Now, do I tell your father I have been speaking to his unborn children? They are perched at the precipice. They are ready.

Your son is quiet. An architectural mind. Your daughter, an artist, a cyclone.

I am homesick for you.

I like things that ghost: pages, people, memory. What else is a ghost besides partial?

Here, we will match you to a body, and the trick will be remembering that this body is housing only. It is just a place to be.

In sleep, I have gone with you to the top of the hill. We are looking out over the peaks, patched with snow. Your dense body, my arms. I do not know how much I do not know.

In the Australian forest, a man kept a pet lyrebird. He played flute songs, which the bird learned, and sang when it was released to the wild. Even now, all these generations later, the birds still sing flute traces of Keel Row.

> *O weel may the keel row,*
> *The keel row, the keel row,*
> *O weel may the keel row,*
> *That my laddie's in.*

It is not theirs, this song they sing.

For a few days, I thought this would be a book about your coming and then your arrival. When you decided not to stay, it became a book about your absence. That is a harder book to write.

Wanting to perfect the art of waiting. The art of being at loose angles with things. The art of the bird in the woods, mimicking the chainsaw, no worry of oblivion.

Today, I woke and imagined leaves, small and green, growing on the image of the stark tree trunks on my wallpaper. It was almost too beautiful to bear.

Some day, when you are in this world and older, you will read with wonder, or suspicion, about these things that were here before you, these things that I tried to save for you so that you would have something of them for yourself.

Now, your father is sleeping. Just the tops of his shoulders, the back of his neck, crumpled hair, a shell's curve of ear.

Not now. He does not hear us.

Two

Try reaching the pines before dark, try looking at the
river. Try again. Try your own passage over the bridge.
Try to behave like a stone. Try to ignore those things
you can see in favor of those you cannot. Try bending
light like the hills do. That currency is all their own.

Now, I have walked the river from both sides.

I admit to wishing the same situation in another time.

Windows, mouths, buttonholes.
　　Frames making use of an absence.

What I want to say is:
  I have been paying better attention for you.
  I notice more.
  This songbook, all memory.

Try loving deeply a person you do not know. Try loving a person who does not yet exist. This, like the coming season, is a matter of faith.

Yesterday, at the hem of the road and the woods, two deer in the snow. What I mean to say is that there are ways to occupy the spaces between worlds. There is always a border.

And the axe allows that there might be two parts in everything.

I turned off each light in the house but the bedside lamp. Pink in the corners of the room. I read to myself aloud under the covers.

I could not limit my crying. I was with you there, not knowing what to think.

Right now, you are mostly memory.

And outside, the water is running downhill slowly all night.

I stripped the paper and sanded the remnants, spackled, and sanded again. Soon, priming. Soon, painting. Stay. This will be a place for you.

The garden where we lay under bare branches.
    "Calm me," I asked.

There is no version of you complete. We wait, in the meantime, to see.

How long must the river be cold before it freezes through? Today, there is only a light trace of snow covering the tracks we have made. Now, we have the chance to make them again.

I imagine your face.

It is not your instrument; it is the closest thing I have.

I learn the weight of you in my arms. When I wake, its absence is full devastation.

Come back in spring; these will be flowers.

Our selves were together and I saw, so clearly, the red light of our circuitry.

Some struggle left the remnant of a wingbeat in the snow.

I could not always pass over it. Sometimes I lay down and let it walk through me.

This is the river, and this is the sound the river makes.

"I'll put together your prescription," the doctor said, "but I want you to understand something. People don't get lost. Objects, memories, yes, but not a person."

He left me sitting there on the table.

At night, your father touches his hands to my back. Suddenly, there are waves, beating in all directions and traveling outward.

"Are you doing something?" I ask.

"You felt it?" he replies.

The swallows always know exactly where they are and

how much space to navigate.

My first memory is of a house with a ghost of its own, though this is something I did not know until later. I wished for a nut from the bowl in front of me while my mother and another woman spoke. All the nuts in shells and no way to crack them.

Through the near window, a summer garden.

Tell me again when it began, this life of yours.

I have the sense that I am speaking through walls to you. When I see you in this world, it will be because we have located a door.

From the night window, the girders do not show, so the bridge is a lit path floating in the dark.

A man has learned to turn his camera to the cemetery. He takes pictures of the graves in the dark; they are thick with steam and populated by points of light.

Your father made a video of me jumping rope under a streetlamp in the warehouse lot, but it was dark enough that all he captured was black, and the slaps of rope on pavement, with my feet following suit.

Today, you are everywhere. We stop under the blossoms of the apple tree—there is half a nut there. The shell's small, heart-shaped hollow.

The first time I had been back to that house since childhood, I stood, cold, at the revolutionary grave. My mother walked the gardens, my father used his camera.

Later, a photo showed a light in the house behind me, shining where no light had been.

Guglielmo Marconi, inventor of the radio, wondered on his deathbed if someone would bring him a hearing aid that would allow him to tune in to the sounds of years past. Though slightly diminished by time and distance, he believed they must still be in existence, out past the stars.

I write these sections then I read them aloud.

And before I go to sleep, I find myself hoping to catch a glimpse of you in my dreams.

Last night, an orange tree grew next to the grey expanse of the warehouse across the street. There were no leaves, but on each branch, and fallen to the ground, an embarrassing profusion of oranges.

The terrarium I made in November, just before the weather came. It sits most days at the head of the bed, and the sugar vine inside grew and grew until one pale leaf approached the top, met it, and exited. I watched as it grew larger and darker and took seven days to decide to pinch it back.

B calls to say she is pregnant.

"How do you feel?" I ask. "What do you think?"

"Plain, simple, abundant happiness," she says.

"Then it's your time…I'm so happy it's your time."

As for me, I hadn't been sure. Another two years, I realized. I had wanted to write a book. I lay in bed, sore-breasted and staring at the wallpaper, and from somewhere I heard you, *Begin*.

A coworker told of a relative who, night after night, dreamt of a dead aunt. She would pass through a wall, and he would try to follow, only to fall back. Then, one night, he passed through too. "I made it through the wall in my dream," he told his wife, with joy. And the next day, he died.

Of course, there are places we will not go until we are invited.

I cried and said to you, "I am not certain that this is the time." But I told you, if you were certain, to come.

I trusted, and I do.

The petals of the tulip tree are heaped in piles on the sidewalk—each one curved in the shape of something absent.

Something has happened. Your father and I can hardly speak. We are cut apart and raw at the edges; he rides away on his motorcycle, and his jacket holds him at the waist, impossibly small.

Once, I drove and he rode. He appeared, so fragile, in my rearview mirror in a phalanx of traffic and I thought, to no one in particular, *Protect him*.

The swallows are out along the canal, and what they are catching they are catching just as fast as it flies at them.

We spent the weekend in the canyon, all gold with the season. We lay on a hill where I looked at him until the facts appeared, and I cried.

"You are so true," I told him. "You are like a bell, shot through with it, positively ringing with truth."

"There is not enough time for all the loving I have to do," I say, and I am stricken with it.

"No, no," your father says, and his skin is pooled with pink and yellow, and the tears on his face are bright. "There is time," he is saying, "there is time, there is time. I am sure of it."

I begin again and the words weigh because I have a hole in me somewhere and have forgotten to breathe. "I think if I use the cup of my days very carefully— each second, each minute, I could just begin to love you enough."

In the columbarium, there is a door you should not touch. The man playing the accordion will set down his instrument and run to close it, saying, "Please do not open it, please. There should be a sign posted. The birds will escape."

It is so easy to see how different things might have

been. That you could be six months in me, windows open, rice on the stove, and the sound of your father's car approaching. Inimitable. Home.

Before I knew him well, your father appeared in a dream at my new address with a gift of Edison bulbs held in his hands like a bouquet, and glowing.

Many nights, I ask you to come. You never do. It is only today that I realize maybe you have. I simply do not recognize you.

There is a photograph of my mother and father at a picnic table; the picnic put away, just a jar of olives between them. Their sweaters match, their faces show the elements from which my own is made.

Because I cannot look at it without knowing, I know it as a picture of my waiting.

My mother by the bathtub, wringing the water out of a fabric of her own making.

Some day, I promise to take a picture of you. The sun will be at your back, and there will be a shadow of your body, pinned to your feet, that is ever so much taller than you are.

"This picture is older than you and older than your shadow," I will say. "I have always known about this picture."

And you will laugh, because it is summer, and because you are a happy child, but mostly because I am not making any sense at all.

There is a time above this time, shaped of waiting, and you live there.

There is a point in the road where the runner turns back—the intersection of a street that was home, and the street that is now. A tree there is dropping cherries to the ground.

Come next week, there will be only stones.

Somewhere before sleep, I see a child, head turned back in laughter, a face that's half my own.

Joy tears through the corridors of my heart.

What I am trying hard to learn is the art of loving it all, of living so that all I am doing is the what of right now. I want to say it is something you told me to do: The art of the plate licked clean.

"What I'm writing," I tell her, "is a memoir about a real person. Someone I don't know."

There is simply no other way to explain it. Today I would have been seven months pregnant. Hand over hand, the kite of you reeling in.

In the evening, I wash my blouse by hand, and what floats out of it is all of the canyon I have brought with me.

We are far from the sea, but I wake at five and the bed is empty and a fog like milk fills the city and all its rooms. My eyes hurt to open because, though it is early, there is a light so thick it weighs.

There is something so wrong about it—the fog, the vacancy of this early hour, your father's absence—that I think I have taken a wrong turn in my sleep and awakened someplace else. Just a few small decisions away from the life I truly live. An error made in dreaming.

Long after midnight, we are still driving up the coast.

"Is the ocean right there?" I ask, but I know. The darkness has its own force.

After the service, we walk behind the altar screen to a place by the rose window. There is a box of tissues and a place to kneel, and while they say their prayers, I speak to you.

Later, I light a candle, and then we must leave. They are barring the doors for night.

In my dream, I still cannot speak to you. I am on the phone with the clairvoyant, and I say, "Is my child here? Are there messages, words, signs I should learn to see?"

At that moment, someone peers into the window, and I pull the curtains in a fearful rush. In my ear, she is saying things that do not answer.

July. Your father rides ahead under a darkening sky, his scarf untied. The wind has pinned the center of it to his chest, while the rest flies out behind like white wings from his shoulder blades. Here and there, a car weaves between us and I think: How close they are to this man I love—this man with the dim tail lights and the jacket full of wind.

My mother cuts an apple in the afternoon, then hides the slices in the living room. They are on the window-sill and behind the lamp and perched on the couch. I have found them all but my hands are too small to keep them together.

I come home and your father is asleep. The door to the room is open and touched by the lights from the city—the place I have just returned from.

He has devised an ingenious nest from the bedding. He is sunk into it soundly.

I lie awake for a long time and listen to his silence, and I think about the things I have been telling my friend—about the places we meet and the places we do not, two planks with an imperfect join. I think about the small sadnesses and the things I will not get and the things I will not give and I know, above it all, like a brightness that penetrates: I love. I want for nothing.

Three

"What are the chances of this happening?" a child on the bike path asks of someone older.

What are the chances of any of it, the trolley rounding the corner, the clouds on the hilltop, your father in his day-glo socks, the tearful talk we have now completed? What are the chances of two of anyone being so right and also not?

Through it all, the bee on the face of the flower, gathering.

Ours are the first two seats on the balcony. When the music begins, my breastbone catches it, following the low notes of the drum. I shudder, I pulse.

"Do you feel it?" I ask, and I tap him there, at the door to his chest.

"No," he says.

No. We are different instruments.

Your father in a white car, a red car, a grey car. Your father on a motorcycle, a different motorcycle, another still, a dirt bike.

"It isn't about speed," he says, "it's about going around corners." I fell in love with a man who loves disappearance, and the engine.

The waitress overhears us discussing the wisteria. "It's white," she says, "the wisteria."

"Did it bloom this year?" I ask—I have heard that, somehow, many did not.

"It did," she says, "it was beautiful. I would have been so sad if it hadn't." She carries our glasses away.

Beyond the gate, the plums are falling. The oldest ones are turning into wine.

"Just because you cannot see them," my dead grandfather is saying, "doesn't mean things aren't happening."

The line is crackling. "Hello?" I say, "Hello? There

is something wrong with the connection."

Today is your due date. Yours and mine and ours.

There are bees all the way home, bees for hours. In a hollow house, someone is hammering, and because I cannot tell where the sound is coming from, it is coming from everywhere.

Suddenly, it is late summer and, instead of mothering you, I am at the beach on my back on a sheet on the sand. We are watching the meteors. Your father has never seen one before, doesn't even know what to look for.

"I think I saw one," he says after a while. "It was so fast. Are they fast?"

"They are fast," I say, "just a tail of light."

And then the freight train passes, bright, grinding, and by then we are all in our minds and someplace else.

Your father is asleep, moving softly in the dreams he will not remember. I think of the museum exhibit:

How to transform a man into a rock or a similar object.
How to represent a river that seems to flow constantly.

I read very slowly, with emphasis, and your father holds the book.

All night, the window and the mirror on the wall have a conversation about light. I wake to a voice and cannot tell if it is a person or the river.

I purchase a cheap, plastic camera that shares my mother's name. I take it with us, bring it up the cliff around my neck. It clicks in a loud and hollow way as the film is being wound.

"How do you like your camera?" the man at the ferry terminal asks. He calls it by name.

He says he prefers glass lenses and I think, but do not say, that I chose this lens specifically because I did not want an image so sharp it replaces memory.

I wake and my mother is up; we're the only ones in the whole hotel. "Shh," she says, "your father's asleep." We sit on the cold edge of the tub and eat the green apple she has quartered. "We're having an apple party—it's our secret."

A year ago at this time, you had not yet appeared. Because no spark of you had shown itself, I had not yet begun to think of myself as a thing filled with possibility.

Holy as a balloon filled with breath.

Holy as a pitcher of milk.

Holy as each ordinary morning.

And in the kitchen, the old radio is playing new songs. Songs for dancing close in dark rooms. Songs still undreamt at the time of its making.

We are crammed in the back seat, S and I. Because it is not truly made for passengers, we are folded up, legs to our chests, necks crooked. "Did you know," she is telling me, "that after a woman becomes pregnant, even if her child is never born, cells remain behind? They fight sickness. They gather like an army." I have felt them. Not an army, but a pageantry of love.

We are driving north, your father and I, and it is the first day of fall because suddenly the rains are here. We have all forgotten about them. There is water on the road and a summer's worth of oil, and the road must be banked because I am talking to your father when suddenly the white tile wall of the tunnel is coming at us.

I am, in this moment, unafraid, because some part of me knows: No, this is not how it ends.

I dream that I am on a city bus and suddenly, I see clearly what each person there is looking forward to. A man close-by will have homemade tomato sauce for dinner. A woman is awaiting a telephone call. Another across the aisle has a book to finish. We cross over a bridge where a crew is rowing, and one of the boys in the boat will sleep with his girlfriend that night for the first time. Every single person on that bus, every person I can see by the river, crossing the street, all of them are moving towards something they love.

I wake and think: I am changed forever.

The East Coast is being battered by the worst storm in a hundred years. Your father is asleep on the couch. It is a simple night. There is a jet overhead, and I am thinking of all the people in it, the loved ones they have left, and the loved ones they are flying towards.

I am the keeper of only one set of remembrances.

Walk home in the other direction, walk from the north, and the street feels like a foreign street, though I am only four blocks from home. A tree with heart-shaped leaves, a tree with two trunks wrapped together, the back of the house where your father has heated the last of yesterday's lunch and eats while standing. I see the poplar tree, gold against the soft, dark sky, and remember the morning when we opened the bedroom door and saw that tree, manufacturing light.

Talk with your children when they are young, a book says. *Ask them when they are infants to remember God, so that once they are speaking, they can remind you of what you have forgotten.*

So this is the evolution of love: We arrive with our hearts wide open but do not remember how to keep them that way.

"Feathers," the clairvoyant says, "your grandmother is saying she will send feathers to you. Keep an eye out for them. They'll appear when you're going the right way."

For weeks, I looked where the leaves piled, on the sidewalks, in the streets. I looked for them in photographs. I sought them out. When I told her, at last, that I hadn't seen one, she laughed.

"Your grandmother says the feathers were hard to

find…she asks if she can try quarters instead?"

They came in coat pockets, on car seats, in the street, in drawers, on desks, in unexpected places. I bought cups of coffee with them and sat across from the deceased with a smile on my face. It was then that I noticed the feathers. Your father keeps them everywhere.

The dream of two years ago, where I walked up the ramp of the Port Authority bus station, late in the night. A man stopped me. "It's Meredith now, isn't it?" he asked, and I did not understand.

"Now?" I asked, and then understood that we had known each other for lifetimes and lifetimes. I wrapped my arms around him and felt the way a sailor must when he kneels to kiss the shore.

We bought two beers at one of the Irish bars. I sat next to him on a barstool as our pints were poured before us, looked over, thought with a relief that encompassed all of me—*Thank God I will never have to explain myself again.*

I woke with the feeling that I had lost the only important thing I had ever had. I walked in loops, up and down 9th Avenue. I called a friend who said, "Of course, of course you will find him."

Your father is not that man. We love so newly and the newness demands words.

Four

You came again.

And then, I went into the kitchen and put on water for tea and felt myself begin to bleed. It was all so complicated. How could I even have hoped to hold any of it in my hands, to comprehend any of it? The best I could do would be to simply surrender myself to whatever would come, to swing wide the doors I had been shutting. The all will be anyway.

The tea was fine and delicate and light—an oolong made of little pearl-shaped beads. The man at the shop had explained that they are rolled by hand. He gestured—two hands atop each other, moving something small between them.

Your father left for work, and I stood in the kitchen with the windows touched by steam and looked out at the shaggy pine. Each needle tipped with a tiny drop of water and each drop lit by the morning sun, looking well-planned and infinitely rare.

The photo of your father on a foreign street, in his dark waxed jacket. Though I did not notice it at the time, the brass snaps have caught the light like planets, beaming it back.

For a long time, I have tried to understand your father, the particular ways of his mind. He is not easy to understand—his methods are not like mine; I am so often in the dark.

Who else thinks like this?

We sit on the couch and listen to the rain, and the lamp sees its double in the window.

"You smell like metal," I tell your father. "Metal and smoke."

"Thank you," he says. He returns to his paper.

All night he has been in the garage cutting the pieces from one car to fit into the holes of another.

We were back on the island again, the island of our first beginning. We were all the same and we were all older and we drove through the forests at night and the darkness leaned in on us from all sides. The mountain and the bracelet of road we had climbed last year, where I stood with the wind right through me and thought of you.

If we keep returning, this place will be written over and over with new stories. Through the pages of the first year, we will read the years that follow.

I felt neither far from you nor near. I felt as close as I could feel to a thing both lost and coming.

We soaked for hours in the outdoor tubs, dashed out for respite in the cold air and watched the pines' dark shadows on the dark water. "Look," we said when the ferry cut across the inlet, lit like a home in the distance.

Your father in his body in the water, the only body he now knows. The body he is good at wearing without shame. I watch his back, his soft arms, the steam rising off them, steady and constant.

"Do you think," I ask, "it is possible for two people who have been together a long time to love each other as much at the end as they did when they began?"

"More," he says. Instant, absolute.

Late, in the café, a young man walks in, his wife behind with their baby in her arms.

"Look!" says the waiter who has been curt all night. "A brand new person!" He approaches with such tenderness. "Look!" he says again, close enough to speak to this sleeping child. "You still remember, don't you? You still know all the secrets. Don't forget them. Don't forget," he whispers. "Remember when you're older and tell us. Tell us where we came from."

The words I woke hallucinating, the words I must have been dreaming because I could not remember how they had been arranged.

The small, satisfied sound of the lipstick blossoms as they fall to the floor.

Our mothers and our mothers' mothers. The nothings we would be without them.

They are planting a grown magnolia tree by the new restaurant. The blossoms will be plate-sized. They will smell strong and sweet and clean. Someday, when you are here, I will hold you up to one and you will be radiant in the face of so much beauty.

Your father is selling a car, another car, the one he has always had. The car I would see him driving in the mornings, back when we would pass on the street. I would think: There he goes again, this man I was just beginning to know. I would stand at the bus stop saying, *Come now, please come*, and he would drive over the bridge just like music and get out of his car as the light turned red and hold me in the street.

"Do not sell this car," I want to say. "Remember in the mornings when the battery was drained, we would push it down the street until the engine choked to a start? Remember how we laughed? Even the sand in the carpets is sand we brought."

Outside, in the dark, a man who thinks he might like this car is borrowing it for the night. He is idling it for a long, long time, and the sound of the engine is nothing but the sound of your father coming home. And then, your father comes home and the sound of his car is still in the street and in my head I am scream-ing at this man outside, I am screaming, *Please, please drive away*.

"To meeting," your father says, his glass at an angle. "To meeting and to waking."

We return to the far coast, the crowds for the holiday. At the corner bar where I worked seven years ago, we have a drink. It has not changed. Seven years ago, your father lived here too, though we did not love the same places.

"Why didn't you come and visit me?" I ask, and I am joking.

He looks at me with sincerity and says, "I didn't know. I didn't know you were here."

I imagine us on an April day, as winter is falling away. He is walking west and I am walking east, but we are still a block from each other. Someone turns. We will never know, but the gears are moving. There are still the small decisions of a decade we must make.

You are not young. That is simply the way you will arrive.

We threw ourselves down that hill, your father flat on the sled on the frozen ground, me atop your father as though he was my sled, and when we reached the bottom we were laughing, we were coughing in the cold, we were at the hinge of the new year, and the moon had cast our shadow on the snow.

I told your father what I believe—that you are here with us when you want to be.

"Now?" he asked.

"Hovering," I said.

It will be part of an agreement we made a long time ago—that I will be your mother and you will be a child to me.

You will watch the crows fly up over the dump one morning in winter and you will love their beauty because they do not yet hold another truth for you.

We will belong to each other in rain and in snow, on bright mornings, through accidents. We will belong to each other with our eyes closed, dreaming, with short, expectant lashes. We will belong to each other in the silences and in our waking.

B's child has been born, safe, in the blizzard. "This is a love that remakes me," she says, but it does not. It does not make her again. It made her from the start. It has simply been refound.

How to wear a love so it does not grow thin. So it lasts us, outlives us.

This was where the world began to get more complicated—because I knew more and understood less.

And all the dream doors opening, the dream rabbits escaping. I am carrying them down the steps by the scruffs of their necks, I am ashamed to admit I cannot save them all.

Your father has fallen asleep, and I am thinking of the hurtful things I've said, imagine pulling them out of him. They emerge from his chest in a thin, black thread, which I wind by hand around a bobbin. I burn the whole thing.

In my sleep, I dream he is teaching me how to tie a knot. It holds together two pieces of fabric and I think, *Yes, I know how to do this*, but then he shows me. He is so good at it, so fast.

Five

You sat with me—do you remember?—you sat with your hands on my shoulders and you asked me how easy it was to be good here.

"It's not easy," I said, "because things are so beautiful and because that's so easy to forget."

When you are here, we will walk down the street slowly, naming the flowers. I can feel you, you know, leaning in to listen.

You know why the people here are so tired? It is the body. The body must do everything. You must choose a vessel and your vessel will pass through mine but the vessel is not us. We will be like water—different portions in different cups but always quite the same.

There is a bar in an old house and upstairs, in what must have been a closet, a narrow bench and a tiny copper table. The walls are painted gold. We sat there on a Saturday, and I took pictures of your father's shadow on the wall, his hair like the crest of a cockatoo. We talked about your coming and around your coming as we sometimes do, because there is a book, this book I want to write first. And then I thought, *How silly, you are the book, and the book is you, and none of this is designed to be finished.*

The world you did not live in, but the world you watched.

Your father is throwing himself around the curves of some wet, little island in the dark.

An old motorcycle.

A piece of road he loves.

You see how it is possible for someone to love someone they have not yet begun to understand.

It was just the two of us on the grasses, and the light

was going but had not yet gone, and the boaters were passing by and waving. I waved back sometimes.

"I only wave at the beautiful boats," I said to your father. "The ones that are old."

And he smiled and told me, "I know."

Everyone we will ever meet is here, on this planet, now, or the people through which those people will come, they are here, on this planet, now, and it becomes so easy to see that everything is so neatly tied together that one touch touches all.

Your father has come home, is clipping his nails in the other room—a clean, meticulous click and the drip of the faucet and tiny pieces of him in crescents at the edge of the sink. This is the big challenge—loving the little things.

I ran in the snow by the rusted bridge, by the bent stems of corn stalks out in the fields. I ran so happy that I lost my breath, and I had to quiet myself, stop myself by the side of the trail and remember to keep this moment.

Do we get to do this? Do we get to dog-ear a moment for ourselves and hold it for later, when we are ready and wanting it again?

It is all the same night over and over again. We are being given the chance to live it.

I will take you down the street and show you the first flowers blooming. I will show you the apple tree that fell one night, and the birds that live there still, and the one apple hung high on a branch there, like an ornament.

Then, I will teach you the names of the shapes of the clouds and show you the star at the center of the apple. I will float with you out into the lake and you will look underwater to see what the fish see. And it will be as though you have always been here, because we have always been here, haven't we? We have always.

The drawing, once loved, which is now not as beautiful. The note I keep meaning to write. The paper is even picked out.

I feel a little dried out. One foot in front of the other. It does not matter so much that this will take time. Of course this will take time. First, I need to rediscover what has been lost.

We are driving back home, your father and I, past the logging lands where the clear cuts show. Here and there on the bald earth are places where a single tree still stands. Volunteers, your father calls them.

There are two standing side by side in the wreckage and I say, "Look, look at those two." And, because we have been fighting, I say, "They love each other."

"Yes," your father tells me, "they are built the same way."

Bare trunks for yards and yards before the branches grow.

We are not built the same way, he and I, and I want to ask him to take me to the station—I will take the train home, I will get there late, but I will leave this car and its silence that weighs.

The woman we see—and whose job it is to help us decide whether or not we should stay together—explains that our work is to manage the differences.

I wonder if you watch these sessions and hope that we will come to a conclusion that means you will be born soon and you can come here to live with us.

I met him at the top of the library, and when I arrived on that balcony, he looked at me hard and said, "Now the library has everything I want." I said nothing to that, couldn't, and saw on the way down that his socks matched the neon of the escalator.

Some people keep their child faces. Even when they are grown and old, their child face is there, barely hidden. I passed a man by the bank, a man who was making his way to the halfway house, and his face was still mostly boy. Weathered and beaten back, he could not hide it.

Your father's face, too. He is the child in the photograph standing by a motorcycle, the smile uncontainable. The first time I saw it, I thought, *Nothing has changed*.

Your father is too hard an object.

Write it over again.

Write from the beginning.

Write that there are beautiful things, too, and they must be chosen.

A single light on the porch up the street. A single plane in the sky. There are people pressed against people in train cars and in airports and the thing about them, the reason for all this, is love. They are finding ways, all of them, every day, of keeping love. And because it does not burn steadily, they spend their days throwing matches into their piles of love to see what they can set on fire. It must be done again, all over again, every day. And, though there are the loves that burn, off and on for decades, there are also the little haphazard loves—the stranger at the window, the server, the friend.

When you arrive, you will see it, see the work of it, see how hard it is in all the daily rains and little winds to keep the fires going. It is the first responsibility. It is the primary work.

The press of his hand on me no longer makes a home. I cannot ask him what has changed because it has changed in me.

Someone has sent into outer space a collection of photographs to document our civilization after it is gone. They are pressed onto a disc of pure gold, which, even now, is orbiting us.

One image is a group of orphaned children seeing the ocean for the first time. They are beaming at the camera, tousled and dusty. They are dipping their feet in a black and lasting sea.

I had gone all over town, to every antique and junk shop. There were no compasses. In the end, the one I found looked nothing like I had hoped, but I bought it because I had been unable to think of another gift and, by this point, I couldn't have walked away from the thing I'd searched so hard for.

Your father, who maintains he knew, before we were together, we'd have children. My impulse to prove him wrong. "Did it ever cross your mind that that might not happen? That I might decide this wasn't right?"

He pauses. "No."

I am alone in the house. I am alone by the tub with my head on the tile and the sound of the last door closing.

The woman in the café braids her hair and, as she braids, I watch. I watch because her hands know themselves and this task—there is a fold and then a tug up to tighten and she keeps going until the very bottom where she ties it off and hangs it over her shoulder. She is older, her hair is grey, she applies a bright lipstick. Her partner comes out of the bathroom and looks at her, the way she has made herself so suddenly beautiful, though she has done it so simply.

Her partner is touched, is delighted by this, and she says, "Look, look at your wonderful lipstick!" The two of them gather their coats and leave while the sun is still shining.

We have sat down today and thought about the things that are left to be done before we invite a child. "Let's try for the fourth quarter," your father says, as though this is a fiscal year or a basketball game.

You will love clocks or maps or searching for stars. You will love making straight lines, or you will love the shapes of things, or you will love digging a spoon into a melon, making curls of its flesh. You will blow bubbles in your water, or you will take small, neat bites of your sandwich crusts, or you will hate bananas unless they are sliced into rounds. You will sweat in your sleep and wake with hair stuck to your face. You will wrap your legs around my waist and hang there, or you will insist on a piggyback ride up the stairs. You will love the grid a screen presses into your skin. You will eat your oats with cinnamon, and, in summer, when you swim, you will always run in all at once.

Six

For a part of it, you were dreaming. For a part of it, you were waking, and you wondered without words where we were and why there were walls there and what work the roofs did. You wondered why we were the people we were because it hadn't always been that way, so the choice was, somehow, arbitrary.

We found the road after all, Steamboat Road, which turned into Young Road, which took us to the park we wanted to find, the beach we were looking for. We had an oyster in a cookie jar—a live oyster we had bought at the Japanese noodle shop, and which I wanted to return home.

We were heading north along the inlet, and the sun was setting beside us. "The light looks like light we are already remembering," I said.

"Hmm," your father replied.

I save the marmalade jars because they make nice glasses for tea and because the lids fit tight. The expiration date is printed on the side and I think, as I look at it, that one day I will look at it again, surprised, to try to remember where I was that year, the seventh of March, and what, since then, has changed.

We watched a collection of footage of cars crashing into each other, over and over, strangely, absurdly. Cars slipping on ice, veering off the road, driving into streetcars, lamp posts, each other. In the last clip, two people collected their items from their crashed vehicle, shut the doors, and simply walked away.

I don't wake looking for something to throw, but I am there soon enough, and so are the rolls of film, and I am hurling them one by one at the side of the stove, hard, where they hit with a loud and hollow sound. I throw all seven and I think that I don't even know what is on these rolls, how old they are, who they belong to.

I leave without shutting the door, without saying goodbye. I want your father to emerge from the bathroom to see that I am gone. I climb the hill fast until I am out of sight.

I have seen a windup machine from 1890—a machine with a tiny crank and bellows that creates a bird song that is light and quick and believable.

Believable to me, but I am not a bird.

"Maybe," your father says, "you don't have to think of this as the worst thing the world over. Maybe you were born for this."

"I will not have children like this," I say. "I will not have a child who cannot express the way he feels. It would kill me. It would kill me."

"You should put that in the book," he says, flatly, because that is the way he speaks.

And it sparks something terrible in me and I say, "I won't put that in the book. There is no book. That's not what the book is about."

I kicked the wall and cried in huge, heaving breaths I thought would break me, and I pushed him as he lay in bed doing nothing, saying nothing.

I lost myself entirely in that moment, I traveled to the bottom of a huge and holy grief, and he sat there and watched.

In my dream, there is a hole in my chest. "Look at this," I tell your father as a paste pours out. "Don't look, don't look!" I cry, and ask him to turn away.

In the morning, your father listens as I tell him this and, after a silence, says, "Even in your dreams, your heart hurts. And you think it is too much for me."

I have made so many mistakes and have so many more.

They want to see if they can build new connections. "Make his emotions connect more efficiently," they say, and I think about the moment on the hillside, lit from within, when he told me how very much he wanted to understand.

I am wading through the water, which is tea-colored with oak leaves. I am swimming out to the raft. I am almost too young to name the fear that seizes me be-

cause I am floating. I am traversing the top of an unknown dark.

"What," I ask carefully, "are some of your happiest
moments?" I wait. "The moments you remember as the
brightest, the most lasting?"

"It doesn't work that way for me," your father
explains. "I don't have memories in my mind, not like
that, not with feelings attached."

I feel as though the garment of our love has been
unzipped, held aloft, and blown away. I cannot keep
myself from asking, "What is the point? What on
earth is the point?"

The notebooks your father gives as presents arrive in
a jacket of glassine which I take pains to preserve.
Inevitably, as I carry them around, the jackets tear, and
then the tears tear and eventually they are too worn
to use anymore.

I love the sound of them. It describes a newness.

What must I expect to sacrifice?

Today, I walked to the café without glimpsing your
father. I passed over a message spray painted onto the

sidewalk: SOWING SEASON. I wondered what that could mean to me, if now were truly a time to be sowing something. What would I be planting? What would I hope to harvest?

I think of the happy moments that are always orbiting us. The sad ones there and orbiting too, a shadow double.

I try to explain your father to a friend. "Most simply," I say, "he has no words for his feelings. He cannot express them. Often, he is unaware they're there at all."

"Then how do you know he loves?" this friend asks.

It was a question I didn't yet know to dread. It is a question I have been asking myself in so many ways for days now, on slow loop. I thought I felt it, but who's to say? It could have been anyone's love. It could have been my own, beamed back.

Serendipity is everywhere, if you want to see it. It seems so clear that everything is tied together so exquisitely and irrevocably with intricate knots. And then, if you decide the situation wasn't meant to be, those perfect coincidences suddenly fall apart and it is so easy to suggest that none of it was ever meant, none of it had to be that way at all.

After a fight on the waterfront, we rode our bikes back downtown, found a Japanese restaurant for our dinner. *Send a postcard to your future!* a sign on our table said. We asked the server, who brought us a card and told us to leave it when we paid. "Someday," she said with a smile, "we'll mail it."

That was in another country, so I wonder. Perhaps it will not be sent. I did not see the message your father wrote and he did not see mine. We have gotten further and further from that moment. I have forgotten altogether what I said.

I have no answers for you. You see there are places where these years of living have taught me nothing at all.

Many times recently, I look at something and catch myself thinking that it would be a good thing to throw. That it would be satisfying in some way, because I can imagine the way it would crash or crumple or break, and that excites me and makes me think, *Yes. That. Do that.*

A widow in London was married to the man whose voice had been used in the underground station's audio memo—*Mind the gap*. Their love had been late-blooming, she said, and the comprehension of the fact that it was late in their lives had given weight to things.

After his death, she would sit in the stations and listen to his voice as the trains boarded. *Mind the gap. Mind the gap.* Sometimes, she admitted, she let two or three trains pass just to hear him again.

The world is astounding. It is, if not everything I want, the frame that reveals everything I want.

Your father sits at the far end of the couch and explains that he hasn't lost any of his love—he simply does not know how to express it. *But you did know*, I think. *You did, you used to. I do not understand how, but you forgot.*

Your father, or perhaps he is not your father, says the words do not come. He has no way of knowing the things he feels, no way of explaining them, even to himself. It all remains in the lockbox of his heart, where it occasionally escapes in the form of a headache, a chest pain, cold hands.

How could I be expected to know anything he

does not know himself?

I open the door and you are lying there in the dark. Your eyes are open. In the light from the hall, they are shining.

How long does it take for two people, once they have been linked, to unlink themselves from each other? It happens, then some morning they wake and their own best reasons have left them.

I have sewn a label onto your father's hat—small, even stitches in red thread. This is an insurance—that if this hat is ever lost, it might find its way back home. It is the only thing I could say your father allows himself to be attached to. The only thing he panics for. I wish I had given it to him. All I could arrange to give is its return.

Seven

I find a bee down by the warehouse. At first, I think it is dead, but then I pick it up and it moves. One leg. I rest it in a flowerbed and, hours later, I pass by again. The bee is still there, motionless.

What to do with a grounded bee, an article reads. I bring this bee indoors and try feeding it a solution of honey and water with a cotton swab. It lies on an atrophied side and does not eat.

"I want to wake to see you fighting," I say, and place a colander over the bowl for the night.

In the morning, the bee has died.

"But what about its spark?" your father surprises

me by asking. "Where did its spark go?"

"It hardly had any spark left," I begin. "Most of it had already gone on to other places."

At first, I think I will make him a list. I will write the moments I remember on a page, one by one, or I will write them on cards and little slips which I will leave for him to find around the house when he least suspects.

That moment when we pulled over by Big Sur, I will write. The plants electric on the hills, the flat ocean. I wore a dark dress with a red print. The wind in our hair.

The photograph of us after our first fight. The silent cathedral, the cold Pacific, the light in that forest —God, it was green—the time I tripped putting my underwear on and fell in a heap on the floor.

Does he not remember? Does he really not remember? I wanted him to have them, too, so he could sing them back to me when I forget.

If it is only my truth, it begins to feel like a lie.

This is a book about memory. It is a book about time. It is a book of the photographs we took and the photographs we lived.

I thought I was remembering these things for you, but it seems they are for your father too.

And if this man is not your father, if, one day, he is simply a man I knew and loved, then what would this book be to him?

Unless they have painted over it, there is a constellation of marks in your father's old home—the place where my feet hit when I stood on my hands.

One fall, we drove to a park in the south of the city. I hardly knew him then. The season was folding; the forest was cold. In the back seat of his ancient car was a pair of cowboy boots and a toy gun. "My Halloween costume," he explained. "I was a cowboy who got shot through the heart."

I sat in the park and the birds called over and over again to each other in the language only they understand. What I heard sounded just like, *You're here. You're here.*

I could have told you anything about the park—the ancient trees that knit their own darkness, the rhododendron that has lopped over to lean on the ground, the thickness of the air because it is dusk and spring and because the season is still hanging.

People are walking through in bright colors and you can imagine it is any evening in summer and that thought—that someday soon it will be light late—makes the whole future feel expansive.

I waited for a long time for the feeling to return.

Every once in a while, it comes back, or I believe I see it. A glimpse.

The day before I left town, I came home to discover that your father had cleaned the house. The floors, the sheets, the shelves. Even the Easter Lilies had been removed. There were yellow tracings where their stamens had stained the sink.

It may be that I have stopped looking for you. You are out there, still, but I am not able to feel it because the rest is too thick.

The sign on the church up the street reads: SELL YOUR CLEVERNESS. BUY BEWILDERMENT.

I travel with the traffic up the hill, all of us sightless in the last half hour of sun.

My mother cuts my hair, and we drape it on branches for the birds to find. "It's nesting season," she explains.

It could have been any wall. Could have been any bridge. I had hoped to find a way in or a way over— had been hoping for years.

In a dream, I labored for two hours, then understood that the labor was over. Only, there was no baby.

From the window, your father and I are watching two crows at the top of a tree. It is a late one—there are not even leaves yet—which is why we can see one sidle to the other, closer, closer, until their shapes merge and it is clear that they are mating. It is quick, it is not particularly beautiful to me, or at least it is less beautiful to me than the moment when they fly away like broken-off pieces of a something that is larger than all.

Across the canal a child calls, "Ready or not, here I come!" and begins to run, and I am trying to remember why it is—and how—that voices carry so well across the water.

And I have the sensation right now that I am falling,

falling, and the people around me are falling, too. How have any of us survived the losses we have lived? If all of us are feeling the things we might be feeling, it is a wonder we have survived at all. I am trying to understand why I feel there is a small earthquake, and I am swaying and swaying as though there is a secret heart beating beneath me and everyone else is just carrying on.

And the sound of the dog in the other room, who is sleeping with his eyes open.

My birthday, a full moon, an eclipse.

We are standing in the street, which is silent because the hour is so late. It is not true that the moon is as bright as day, not as they say, but it is still a presence that paints things.

We are looking at our house, at the stillness of the intersections and your father is watching the time saying, "Not yet. Not quite yet." Until it is midnight and he says, "Happy birthday," and holds me.

Your father forgot to make a wish. I lit all the candles and sang to him again and he closed his eyes and took a deep breath and said, "Wait!" and his eyes snapped open. "Can I change my wish?"

"You haven't made it yet," I said.

He closed his eyes and breathed in, and once more his eyes opened wide and he asked, "Can I change it again?"

"Take your time," I told him, and he blew out all his candles then, just barely, with the last of a breath.

We have gone to the desert. We are watching the stars. There are so many more of them here than at home and they puncture what would otherwise be a clean dark.

We are remembering what is written about stars— that their light takes hundreds of years to reach us.

"These stars we are looking at, they may have burned out," one of us says. And we stay there and we fathom this with the crickets in the dark. Far off, someone has put on a song for dancing and it finds us there, at the edge of the wilderness.

I wonder how many of these stars have died. I understand there is no way to know.

The oasis, which seems less beautiful when I discover the waterline and know it is maintained.

We returned to the place where we had made our nest

of grasses. This year, they are lower, the canyon dry.

Your father's hands are cold. He is pulling a tea strainer from his bag, opening it, going through the leaves with his fingers, holding up a ring.

He is asking me to marry him, and this moment is pulsing in me with a beat of disbelief.

"Yes," I say, and then, "do you want this?"

Eight

There is a fountain by the desert's edge. You can wash the dust from your face there, but the water is warm.

The woman at the back of the stage is manufacturing a gale. It goes with the picture of the mountains there. It is a certain, cold, kind of wind.

"Sometimes the choices will be illogical," sings the woman at the piano, "commit to the wrong road."

And then, he puts the flame in the box and steps inside.

A famous cinematographer had said, "We need a lighthouse, an orphanage, and a swamp. But if we can't have those, we can use a room all painted black with some lights."

They found him what he needed, but I would have liked to know how it would have worked otherwise—the makeshift.

I enter, floating, and the night is as dark as the water, and the webs of light stretch as far as the river stretches and I, though afraid, am part of it.

Also, a rope of rough fibers that descends from the surface to the bottom. It is lit from a spotlight at the top, and the bright rope is all that is visible in the water for some distance until the light's reach ends, and the rope continues in darkness.

In some way, we will never be able to escape the loves of our past. I suppose I cling to them, and this clinging is because there is something I still want there.

The lanterns above glow red, and the stereo plays to just us in the empty place, a song about what used to be. Your father knocks the last half-glass of his champagne to the floor.

There, on the road that goes into the woods, two deer, staring back.

Having forgotten last night's dreams except that there were women in contests of their own making.

This new decision we had made, I stumbled around inside it, seeing how it might fit. We went down the street to celebrate at a restaurant that overlooked the creek. Your father ordered rabbit, and when it came, the coyote came, walking right down the seam of the dry creek bed. He watched us and we watched back, and then he went off and howled in the canyon somewhere.

He had made the night into two nights—the one we had had before and the one after.

The ring is sterling, it is soft, it has taken on the impression of what has happened since.

Your father is at the countertop, buttering a piece of toast. I watch him, in a shirt he rarely wears and something changes and suddenly he is unfamiliar. A stranger.

I am staring, he is speaking, it is as though our whole history has fallen away, and I am seeing anew again.

A *yes*. A large and certain *yes*, or a smaller *yes*, or a *yes* that is more simply not a *no*. There are these kinds of affirmation.

At first I spoke to you wildly and often because I had to. Because you were the other person in the room and, before that, our silence was long. Now, I run the risk of having nothing left to say. You are lost to me.

Do not despair. It is only a body.

For better, for worse, for richer, for poorer—it is a statement whose beauty derives from the fact that no one has any idea how much they are signing up for.

Your father had brought a bar of chocolate to the desert—a fancy one, which he left in the car. By the time he remembered, it had melted to a sauce inside its wrapping.

"Is it ruined?" he asked.

"No," I said. "Let's save it."

I eat it now by sucking the chocolate away and spitting out the gold that's left on my tongue.

But the hills looked like that—they actually did. Every

single one of the grasses was lit, and your father was running up a little slope, suspended for a moment.

But even my memory is not as beautiful as that photograph.

Please, speak to me in my dreams.

And that I will remember them.

It was like turning a corner into sunlight.

I was on my back in the dark room and you appeared, turned in profile, an oval face, waves in your hair, a beautiful and serious smile on your face. *Who is the man in the corner?* I thought. At first, I did not know.

We are motorcycling home on the old viaduct, the one they will destroy, north, and the sun setting on the water by the mountains and the cranes and the cargo ship and the Ferris wheel, still circling though all its lights are out. Each swinging carriage, rising and falling.

In the tunnel, the lights cast us in shadow. Your father's knuckles are flickering under the sodium lamps, shaking with the engine. The tufts of hair that his helmet won't cover smell like sweat, long day, gasoline.

I will never understand him, I think. *Never com-*

pletely. He will always be a mystery. My own helmet is busy casting the reflection of my eye, faint and enormous, over all.

When you came, you came as a man. I wondered why you were there in the corner of the room, and then I noticed your face.

When you came, you were there all at once, and I pressed my face into the place where your neck meets your shoulder and you held me. I beamed as I cried and I thought, *You are so tall now, look how tall you are*, and we held each other in the way that a hello and a parting share.

"It is not now, not now, not quite now, but please return, please return," I said to you. And you receded then, quite simply, like the fading of a light. You have not been present since.

I am still second-guessing. Every decision for something amounts to a decision against something else.

"In my religion, we have a saying," the doctor says. "What hits you, there was no way it would have missed you. What misses you, there was no way it would have hit. The story is already written. The ink already dry."

I had hoped your father would come to the café with me. I turned the clock upside-down so he would not realize what time it was.

Your father has come home late. He has washed all the metal filings from his hair, and we lie in the dark and talk of marriage.

There is no perfect person. I am thinking of this— that the perfect person does not exist, though there must be, purely mathematically, a person who is *best*— when he says, from the dark beside me, "Don't you think there is a resonance between us?"

"A resonance?"

"A vibration."

"What do you mean, a vibration?"

"An energy. It enlivens us."

For a moment, I am quiet.

"Where does it come from?"

"From inside you," your father says. "From inside me, too."

Your father has just sent a picture of me swimming

on the hotel roof. Just my feet above the water. SWAN, he has called it.

It was around that time we started to smell like each other.

"It always reminds me of you," your father says.
    "How is that?" I ask.
    "The part about the heart."

Nine

Someone is dancing there, with a kite. He is standing in the spoon of the hillside, letting the string out, then reeling it in. He cuts close to the people there, but he does not want to talk with them. He wants to be there wordlessly.

Even as I am saying it, I know it is unkind. It wasn't what I had wanted, but I am there now and there is too much momentum behind the thought for me to let it drop.

I wanted—want always—to dream about you, though

I do not. Instead, I dream that I am waiting tables, and a man is asking me if there is a white wine on the menu that is crisp, light, green-tasting.

"I like a wine," he says, "that makes me sing when I drink it—*Figaro, Figaro, Figaro, Figaro*." He gets louder and louder, and more and more animated.

We are at the races watching men throw themselves around corners with precision and ferocity. The cars are old but they have been beautifully maintained. Now, there is nothing old about them but the shapes. The insides and the engine bays are pure gloss white.

"So the damage shows," your father says. I ask if the cars can ever be fixed once they are crashed and your father says immediately, without thought, "Whatever is made by man can be restored by man."

The Mexican restaurant has a stack of business cards by the door. There are lotería symbols on the back. I shuffle them, face down. "Pick one," I tell your father.

The harp. *Old ways of doing things are no longer useful.*

The frog, I choose. *It is just a little thing, nothing to be scared of.*

In my dreams, strangers talk with your father. They

are old friends, it seems. He tells them that we are getting married and they are congratulatory. He tells them that I am indecisive and they look at me.

"He is a good man," they say. They do not try to convince me. They let the fact stand.

We walk up the street in the dark. It is that hour when the lights are on, and the night has come, and the people in each house are visible to us.

"Look!" says your father as we pass. "A library!" He is not excited for himself. He is excited for me.

Your father wanted ice cream for dinner. He wanted a walk. He wanted to read on the couch while I went to bed. The city was lit before us, the moon was full, it was at an apogee and we stared.

"Well," she says, "memory also is not to be trusted."

The fledgling was still there when I returned, so we threw a blanket over him and put him in a box and brought him home.

He slept. I peered in the box to see and only once did a bright eye stare back.

In the morning, we returned him. He stepped out

of the box into the light and began to call, and they came for him, came from far off to find him—they had thought he was gone.

"I hate to admit this," your father says, "but the days are getting shorter. Coming home tonight, I could tell." He waits. "I thought there were more days left."

I want to say I knew there would be differences, I just did not expect them to be these. These, so unmanageable.

"Yes," she says knowingly, "the hardships are always the ones you would avoid. Anything, anything but these."

I want to tell her that I have been crying alone at the table of the Indian restaurant for a love I can recognize.

We leave the bedroom door ajar and it is either a streetlamp or the moon that reaches around and makes a flag of light.

This is how the morning happens: People wake and put their minds to it.

When we came home, he stood silent in the kitchen. I held him. "I love you," I told him. "I love everything about you even though you don't always make sense to me. I'm working for this. I'm really working for this."

He cried, and he shook as he cried. "It might be easier with someone else."

"Yes, but I'm trying it with you."

The shape of your father's hat in the corner, folded and expectant. It startles me because I so sincerely assume him to be with it.

"A child," she says, "with your eyes."

There is a chapel in the airport—a simple room with pastedown carpet and a boxy altar. Everywhere the priest's chair has been moved, it has left a mark along the wall. Even with the sounds of luggage outside, it is calm inside. There is a real candle burning.

Yesterday, a man came down the road in the jacket your father wears—blue quilted chambray—and it stopped me cold. I had the urge to hug him without introduction, without explanation.

A sigh that carried through the house. The moon through the curtains. And your father, who often cannot sleep, calling through his falling and his falling fast, "Will I see you in the morning?"

"Yes," I say. "Yes, there is time."

And the light of the moon through the window and your father on his back in the bed, breathing deeply now, and a thought that comes to me completely unbidden, *Take the gift that is given.*

I write it down on this page in the dark.

And we will have, in our yard, a pine tree and a pear tree, whose fruit we will ripen on the windowsill. You will come down in the morning and choose one for your breakfast, and you will eat it in the kitchen dripping juice upon the floor—each drop as final as a statement, and as sure.

"I don't know what year it is where you are," she had said, "but it's 1942 where I am."

I taught your father how to sit in a canoe—how to get in and how to get out. Put your hands on the gunnels; keep your center of gravity very low. Learn to move with the boat.

I admit I loved him as I wanted to be loved.

I didn't know an other way.

During the storm, the seaplanes begin to return home
—suddenly, from all directions—like animals when
the season calls.

Remind me not to forget.

"You'll drop it," your father says.

I am determined not to. I loop around, I learn the
weight of it, how to make it turn, until I make too
sharp a maneuver. The motorcycle drops between my
legs—there is not enough time for the kill switch.

"Good." He says, "Now you know it's nothing to
be afraid of." I'm so shaken, and the tank is so full, I
cannot even lift it on my own.

The chair at the top of the stairs where we remove
our shoes.

Our mismatched cups.

The plant that needs to be watered. The plant that
does not.

"What's the occasion?" asks the florist, and the question does not seem entirely professional. He means—*Why are you sending him flowers in the middle of a workday afternoon?* I do not say it is because we have fought, that I have told the recipient of these flowers that I do not think we should be marrying. I do not say anything. "Is it just because?" the florist asks, graciously.

Ten

"To understanding." I raise my glass.

"To great understanding," your father returns.

And I walk again under the horse chestnut, leaves thrown to the ground, and I think of the nothing and the everything that has changed.

The city has been, for days, covered with the kind of fog that makes everything feel at a distance, apart. I walk past a bush where there are birds nested inside and singing. I come closer but the singing stops and I am left there, on the sidewalk, staring into silence.

"I was swimming," I said, "when you woke me."

"Lake Union?" he asks, "Hundred Acre Pond? The Sound? The Ganges?"

"No, a dream water."

This was your father's door. This was the code that opened it.

The morning, the hard morning, when the fog has not thinned, and the masts of boats still disappear into it. I sleep between alarms and wake full of the dreams I have had—dreams that are clipped short and squeezed into space.

I am guilty of wanting a simple and beautiful life.

"Tell me more," says a voice at the edge of the known. I had been sitting on the floor trying to find you again. I had been imagining your body in my arms. I had to build it all myself—the image, the breath, and the weight.

She reminded me that there had been a time when I had told her, "There is nothing I don't like about him."

"But you know," your father had said, "there's something wrong with everyone."

"What about you?" I had asked. "What's wrong with you?"

"If you don't know by now," he had said, "I'm not telling."

"Tea?" I ask.

"No, no tea. Is this a peace offering?"

For months after, we would see crows on the telephone wires and ask each other with humor but mostly sincerity, "Do you think that's our boy?"

Knowing he had long since lost his fledgling call and that his grey eyes had gone black. There is no way to recognize him now.

The plant I found out by the trash, lopped over and faded, has sent up new growth.

"I knew it would," I tell your father. "It just wanted to be taken seriously."

The truth is, I did not know for certain I could save it. I am forever throwing my faith at things.

"I broke a glass," your father says, defeated.

"What would make today better?" I ask, seating him at the table.

"Tomorrow," he says.

We have gone through the house finding each of the clocks and changing them back. Some storm is blowing the leaves from the trees, tearing off the weaker growth, washing the water over the bridge. The radio says that, all across the city, power lines are down. People are sitting in the dark.

"What happened to our summer happened to our knives," your father says. It is true; our knives need sharpening.

I walked out into the wet street with just socks on my feet. I threw myself in front of the car. I gave back the ring.

After crying, I slept, balanced on the edge of night. It was cold and thin and it stung to lie there listening as no car came. He had disappeared. The leaves on the trees trembled and then fell with a tenderness that was neither fear nor faith.

"Your hardness will be the end of us," I had told your

father as he readied to leave.

"Okay," he had said. *Okay*.

I have propped the painting of waves up on the ledge of the radiator so the houseplants can contemplate the sea.

"I like the way the couch is decaying," your father says.

"What do you mean?"

"There are all these hidden threads."

A man on the news has a pet bison, and it is pictured in his living room—the creature so large it disturbs the scale of things: the man, the room, the furniture.

"Let's get a bison," I tell your father.

"Are we breaking up or getting a pet?"

"Just imagine it," I say, "something so much bigger than us."

Your father reminds me that I cannot leave him until the book is finished.

"But you are pre-supposing," I say, "that you are in the book when it ends. Even I don't know that. I could write a different ending. There are so many endings."

Perhaps I am staying for you. Because I have already

seen your face. Because I do not want it to change.

At the elementary school, the gate is open. The gate is open and there is a thin, black glove at the foot of the steps.

I walk up both flights and look in the windows at the names of the students on the walls. Each name an infinite story.

November, and it is possible to imagine that it is the moon that is moving and the clouds which are still.

Perhaps, I thought, *my feelings are as foreign to him as his thoughts are to me*.

It was like the loosening of one side of a lid.

Eleven

I brewed a strong cup of tea but did not drink it. I set the timer and lay on the couch with the teabags on my eyes, and I waited. I waited for the puffiness to fade, I waited to look like something other than a woman who had cried until she was emptied.

We do not keep the salt in that bowl any more. It weeps, and then corrodes.

The house is not made for cold like this. It comes through the floorboards and the walls and the windows and is everywhere all at once.

They are explaining that we usually get our weather from the west, but lately it is coming from the north. Even our skies have changed.

There is a flock of songbirds over the dump, swooping and weaving through the cold, dry air. To one side of the skyline and back again. Dawn is still coming. Because they have been doing it for so long now, not going anywhere, it simply seems an exercise in joy.

We lie in bed, and I talk and cry and look at his small, square hands on the bedcovers. He says very little, and I try to stop myself from saying all. The sharp winter sun is fading the books on the shelf. I can no longer speak kindly.

This morning, the city is fumbling over and over again in the fog. The small, thin chimneys are putting out smoke and there is the suggestion of a light in the east, though the denseness of the sky does not change.

Good morning to you. Good morning to you with the stars still turning and the all-possible day. I have not yet decided what to do with it.

There is a little school around the corner, and every

morning, parents wheel and walk and carry their children there for the day. It is overhung by a big pine; smoke streams from the chimney. Suddenly, I am filled with a longing for you. I will know how to love and what to teach.

We know how to do the most important work without instruction. It is the little things that throw us.

We have forgotten. We have so successfully forgotten that we question much and believe little and do not feel ourselves carried along by anything. And there the birds are again, out at the horizon, going nowhere exactly, but doing it with grace.

In a dream, we are getting married, though we don't. I wake before it happens.

Sign outside the used car lot: *All this year must go.*

It was just me, singing for courage in the dark.

In my dream, my last dream, the dream between alarms, we walked around the lake in the sun. I wanted to make a wreath of evergreen. I called the plants by name.

An apple tree, more of a lanky sapling, was bowed to the ground under the weight of its oversized fruit. It took both hands to hold one.

We are not yet at the shortest day of the year. We are still heading into darkness, and our days are clipped a little more as they come.

Orion's cold belt above us. We have driven off the ferry in the dark and now, on the island's only road, we are part of the parade of arrivals. Tail lights and tail lights and then ours too, heading for home.

I loved, or I wanted to love, the sun coming in at the edge of the window, the frost it melted, the spider's web it illuminated. I loved or I wanted to love, and those feelings I understood would be difficult to tell apart.

Which is more beautiful: The object which does many things, or the object which does but one? All I know is how grateful the latter must be for a need it can fill.

I will be there with my mother, counting the buttons on my shirt, telling a part of my future—*Tinker, Tailor, Soldier, Sailor, Rich Man, Poor Man, Beggar Man, Thief.*

And the song that was playing all over the city, it was there at some point in its progression wherever we were, and when we ran into the teahouse to escape the cold, it was just hitting the chorus. The unison.

Those bright years of ours were also true, and there is a pocket somewhere where they are still present, still playing themselves out, and our old selves are there, much to their delight.

The sun is up, just up, just over us, turning the sheets to rags, our bodies to rags. The sky is pink, pink even though I am still half-asleep. I cannot compare.

The paths that have changed, the paths that have not. The fox barks in the woods, and the night sharpens.
    Home. The spots on the floor from a dog now dead.

Stand in the garden and look at the stars.

I did not have a camera, so I asked myself to remember.

They ask when the wedding is. They ask outright, or they ask in a way that is hidden, but they all want to know. I cannot tell them that I am wrestling with it. I am afraid to be left wanting.

The tenement windows just outside the city. Lit in the night and for each light there is a person: disappointed, calm, angry, tired, waiting, dying, filled with hope.

Eve of the new year. Bitter cold city. I sit by the café window, bring the soup bowl to my lips. Someone in the park across the street is sailing high on a swing-set in the dark.

At least one keyhole has been stuffed with tissue by a previous tenant. So there is no seeing through.

A very partial morning. The things I am trying constantly to re-make, alter, edit, adjust. Bring myself back to the path, and the path is hard to find. I do not always want it.

The early morning young mothers' parade. A child I cannot see, screaming, "I need it! Give me!" The complete anguish of wanting.

A soft rain is falling, so fine it looks like dust in the air around us, and everyone holds their umbrellas like a gift.

The knives come back sharper than they had ever been
—sharper than new. We arranged them in the kitchen
like an arsenal. We were afraid to put them away.

"What is your favorite place?" I asked the tree.

The place where I am.

Twelve

I admit I had thought things would be, somehow, vaster.

Thinking I had dropped something. And I had. What was it? It was the key.

"What if," she suggests, "you could feel two conflicting things at once. The loving and the wanting to leave. Could you hold them both?"

Astonishingly, it does not break me. I am the dish that holds both hot and cold.

Can I tell you something? Can I tell you something

and ask you to hold it very close, like an egg or an instrument?

I have a leaf in my heart.
    You have a leaf in your heart, and I want it.

I have fallen hugely and heavily into not knowing. I am as made of it as a balloon is made of air—a thing that is simply a container for something else.

In what other world do I live with you? In what other world do I wake with you? In what other world could I feel more longing than I do for the things I do not have, the things that may not even be possible, but that has not stopped me from wanting them.

"My girl," your father says, "I'm sorry, but our keys slept together all night."
    "They did? Did they dream about doors?"
    "No, they dreamt about keyholes."

This is how it happens: Everything is, for a moment, less precious and then, for a moment, more. That is how you know you are leaving each other.

What was it but a gradual unfolding from a dream, a dream from which I hadn't wanted to awaken?

Or perhaps, I am not your mother. Just someone who speaks to you.

There is work to be done. You can either fight it and let it break you or embrace it and let it break you.

The arboretum is cold and damp. We reach it by the narrow footbridge across the access road. The lamps have not yet been switched on for night, and there are other visitors there, walking in the dusk. "This is a museum," your father says, "in case we kill all the trees."

"In my dream," your father says, "I was a giant, golden hand. I tried to catch all the things that flew towards me, but I could never get them all."

The cyclist comes towards us in the mist. Over the bridge. The lamp mounted on her front wheel glows faint and warm.

"I always like lights like that. On the front wheel."
"But they make you go slower," I say.
"There's time."

"I feel there is not."

"I know."

Each day now unfolds strangely. Like any grief, I wake with a feeling of possibility, until I remember that we are lost to each other.

And then I go with him to look at an apartment he thinks he may rent. The hallways smell like cheap perfume, and there are speakers on the outside deck disguised as rocks.

"They're motion-sensitive," says the man who is showing us around. He moves and they begin to play. A sorry background music.

I work to remind myself that I don't hate this man. I don't even hate the building, though it is one I disliked from the moment they began constructing it. What I hate is helping your father find a way to leave.

"Here's a strange news item," your father says. "A town in Tibet has burned to the ground."

"Which town?" I ask. The pictures show an inferno.

"Shangri-La," he says.

"Shangri-La?" I am incredulous.

"Yes. You've heard of it?"

There was a bald eagle, calling to another not far off. It was a high and sharp and lonely sound, and there were two of them.

We watched them drop into their tree like one shadow into another shadow, and I tried to call them out with a song of my own—which did not persuade them because it was not, in fact, their language.

"This is not the book I thought I'd be writing," I tell your father. It sounds at once both pleading and selfish, and I realize what I had wanted to say was that this is not the life I had thought we would be living.

"Fundamentally," says the man at the bar, "they're teaching the kids all this history, but I want them to get back to the truth. The most important thing. The beginning."

I am nodding, imagining a nobody, a nowhere, a dark.

I got a room for the night, downtown. I didn't care about the view or that I could see the waterfront or the city's biggest tourist attractions or that, four stories down and across the street, a woman in some kind of waiting room sat, legs crossed, not visible from her waist up.

On the heavy hotel desk there is a small binder of safety and security procedures:

If the door is hot and there is smoke in the hall, don't panic, you can remain inside and still survive.

If there is smoke outside the window, do not open it—you will not be able to close a broken window.

Memorize the layout of the room; remember how to unlock the door in the dark.

Thirteen

"There are two ways of traveling," says the man behind me, but it is loud and I lose the thread of the conversation before I can hear him explain what these ways are. What is the difference?

I can feel, when I focus, what it was she had said—that I am pressed in on all sides by love. The problem is, that does not fix things—it is simply a sweater in the storm.

I imagine the things I will say:
  You have a barrier to love.
  You have a barrier to believing.

You doubt that I am in this with you, and because you do not trust, you make it true.

I am imperfect, but I wanted you.

And they named themselves as they appeared: angel of hope, angel of clarity, angel of new momentum, angel of understanding, angel of progress, angel of remembrance, angel of comfort in the dark.

What it would or wouldn't have been, what we could or couldn't have done about it, whether or not you were there, perhaps watching us with sorrow, perhaps with comprehension.

These were only some of the things I didn't know, and I could feel the weight of them pressing in on the few things I was certain of.

It would have been easier if I hadn't loved him so much. The love was huge and had room for nearly everything—complications, setbacks, defeat.

Was it not quite large enough?

It is already Friday, it is already Saturday, it is already Sunday. It is already ten years, it is already twenty, it is already twenty-five.

I realized how precious time was for thinking. I realized time was my constraint and my collaborator. I realized there was work to do.

Your father has brought home a bunch of grapes. Perfect grapes, twice as large as any others I have seen. He has laid them across two bowls because just one will not contain them.

I have received no clarity. What seems to be happening is the wholesale unraveling of all the things I had hoped for—entire landscapes and lifetimes heaped back where they came from. Now, they do not fit into those places. It is like trying to make a child disappear.

A part of this book won a prize, will be published. They have asked for a picture of me to appear alongside it.

Your father takes it, though either he is not your father or I am not your mother. He arranges the lights and sets up the camera patiently with his square and capable hands. He tries to make me smile. My hair is down, my hair is up. "Be an owl," he says. "Be a bat," and I make wide-eyed and droll expressions.

In the end, I am not smiling. Not in the shot we

choose. He blows up the picture quite large and dodges in some shadow and brightens the whites of my eyes.

My face on the screen is larger than my face. It is an embarrassment to be touched this way, to be seen so closely, to be revised.

"I'm doing this not because you're imperfect," he says, "but to eliminate the background noise."

"He may pull your violin apart," she says. "Don't worry, he knows what needs to be done."

The repairman comes in, with the detachment of a master. He examines the instrument, he nods, he breaks it at the neck.

"Even so," I tell her later, "I was not prepared."

"Let me polish your boots," your father is always asking me. "Please let me polish your boots. They are not as black as you believe them to be. They are not as black as you remember."

Now, I look down and discover this is true. Entire layers of them are rubbed away.

What did we start out to want? And what did we end up wanting? Where did we find ourselves? Was it what we were planning for? What were we capable of doing and what, in the end, was beyond our capacity?

I read that scientists up and down the coast are finding starfish stricken with a new disease. It causes their arms to twist and writhe and—eventually—walk away from their bodies. Unable to generate new ones, the starfish die.

At the bottom of the article, someone has commented: "I think I have this."

My whole body thinks, *Me too*.

The doctor took my pulse and looked up.

"Some nervousness," he noted.

"We're breaking up," I said.

He looked stricken. As though he had been shoved. "Whose idea was that?" I pointed my finger at the center of my chest and cried.

The door to the warehouse was open and they were building inside it. Greek columns and cypress trees and rose vines climbing. "Props for the ballet," they had told me a long time ago. I hadn't expected worlds.

Someone at my office has discovered an old box of pencils. I took several and now they are scattered around the house: the drawers, the bedside table, the desk, the kitchen. Each one is stamped in foil with the same words: *Between today and tomorrow, life lies waiting.*

They have begun to feel like accusatory fingers pointing. I can hardly wait for the time when each has been sharpened down to a stub and they simply say: *life lies waiting, lies waiting, waiting.*

Children. Children carried by their mothers, wrapped in blankets, walking in boots and hats. Opening the gate.

I try to remind myself what she had said: That I will have children, that they will come, will wait, are not lost to me if this relationship is lost. But I lose the thought, I drop it ten times a day down the well of my worry, which I must then climb down into to retrieve it.

Sometimes, I still feel it. I feel you leaning in close: a symbol, a current, a wave.

"Do you know what you can make with this machine?" your father asked. He waited. "This machine!" His delight is evident.

Your father and I compare sorrows.

"The one I wake with," I say, "that hits me like an urge to scream when I remember who I am and what is happening."

"I don't have that one," he says. "Mine comes in glassy-eyed form."

"What about the one where your heart drops. Where there's pressure on your chest and it seems that everything inside you is falling and falling?"

"That one?" he says. "That comes on throughout the day. I thought it was panic."

Gradually this became a book about losing the things I wanted. It became a book about the things beyond reach and the things that walk away. It was not the book I intended to write. It was the book that wrote itself around me.

Fourteen

J wrote so kindly of my work. "What is interesting," she began, "is that you can convert time from a pinpoint to a square shape—a square as large as a room! This is a powerful talent," she continued, "and therefore, I think you can write almost anything into being!"

This last part, written in pink. My mind clings to it with necessity and longing.

And by the plum tree, not yet blooming, not even leafing out, I thought, *The first step to untying the knots is not minding that it must be done.*

Even the pencil, who makes a life of making itself useful, makes itself useful by disappearing. It lays down a trail of its own substance until there is nothing left, or it is too small to use. And it hopes that, by then, the story has been told.

The flamenco dancer who has brought her own floor. Who will, later tonight, hang her sweaty dress on a hanger.

She is turning faster and faster. She is dancing the flower right out of her hair.

Are we yet at the point where the pendulum will start to swing back?

Your father has taken my shoes out to polish before the conference. "No one will take you seriously with these," he says.

"But I love them," I say.

"It doesn't look like it."

When I woke, I saw that the canyon had not burned, but that our fire had—as your father said it would—simply gone out.

We traveled south. And as we fell asleep, I told him, "Today was a good day. I jumped a fence and stole a lemon from a stranger's lemon tree."

What a hard life the woodpecker has, I thought, as I watched it hopping upside down, drilling against the side of the tree.

I heard the shower turn on, the traffic pass. The shower stopped. After a moment, your father found a glass and filled it.

The woodpecker did not stop.

The eye doctor has me stare ahead into a pen light, which turns into a pillar of brightest white and then green, and then the branchwork of my veins begins to show.

"Eyes open," she says, though they are, already. "A good thing," she continues, "you grew up outside. Your eyes have distance vision. Those of us who stay indoors, we lose our infinity."

A plane has disappeared—simply off the map.

There was no distress call, and so people are calling it a hijacking, a conspiracy, forgetting that it is always possible for something huge and valuable and even loved to vanish.

In the end, in this middle of an end, your father is sick. I have started calling him that again—*your father*—because the facts are unknown and the future is long.

I have watched him slump into fatigue, and he cannot eat and he cannot sleep and bit by bit, like watching a fire die, his light has gone and then his heat.

I take care of him and cook for him and listen to his sadness which is, like mine, a sadness of no answers. I count the grey hairs in his beard.

"Six," I say, "you have six grey hairs."

"What should I do with them?" he asks.

"Keep them. They're yours."

It got harder. Harder to feel you, harder to believe in you. Though it seems insulting to tell a person, *I cannot believe in you anymore*. An insult to the very fact of them.

She asked if I want children, and it cut through me because I wouldn't have said it that way. I would have said that I have children already, and I am seeking a way to bring them here.

Your father is pale and quiet. For the first time, I

worry, because whatever is wrong is speaking louder than he is.

No one has promised us the things we want.

It may be true that all mornings are beautiful, but some mornings are much more beautiful than others.

The potter is so good at what he does, so elegant, that he summons a vase from his ball of clay like a simple fact. As though it has always been there.

I fumble, my clay spins off-center.

"Like this," he says, moving to touch my hands. "Can I?" And he is shaping something there in the middle of the wheel, just by touching me.

I had wanted to go back to the canyon and nail the ring to a tree. To say we didn't know enough about what we were doing but if, in the future, we decided we wanted it again, we knew where it could be found.

But we woke up that day and your father was too tired to move. We did not walk to the canyon at all.

Later, we drove through it, on our way out. I asked him to pull over so I could stand in the heat at the side of the road with the vultures and the sagebrush and the far-off sea.

"I don't know how," your father said. "I'm not a com-municator."

Everyone is a communicator, I should have said, but I told him instead it was a poor excuse.

The plum tree is beginning to flower. Last summer we passed by on a motorbike, on our way elsewhere, and I tapped your father on the shoulder to stop.

More plums on the ground than plums on the tree, but I found a few and we ate them, with our helmets cracked open, each fruit as warm and vital as a heart.

A physicist had devoted much of his life's work to a certain theory of how the world came to be. Thirty years after his initial hypothesis, someone came to his home to deliver the news: Particles had been found to prove that his theory was correct.

In the video, he is calm and quiet with happiness. "All these years," I hear him say slowly, "I didn't know whether I believed it because it was beautiful or because it was true."

I admit that maybe I'm not asking the right questions.

Maybe I don't even know what the questions are.

"What else," the doctor asks, "what other symptoms?"

"Well," I tell him, "my eyelashes are falling out—several a day each day for weeks."

"Are you crying a lot?"

"No," I say. "Surprisingly, no."

Of course, by then, I suspected I was staying with your father because I wanted you. I already knew your face.

I have been losing your father for longer than I have not. The ache that is known.

In a dream, pulling off the dead leaves, telling the houseplants, *You don't need these any more.*

And doesn't it seem strange that I would desire something that I cannot, in the end, even find for myself? That I would be hurt forever by the margin between the life I want and the life I have?

I have a job for you here: Wash the rice until the water runs clear. Like any job, you will like it best if you are not thinking of anything else.

"When will the book be finished?" I had asked.

"Spring," she had said, but she hadn't said which spring.

Truthfully, there is a lot of love. We just don't know quite what to do with it anymore.

I moved over in the bed because I didn't want to be touched.

Will you help me to open the gate? Will you help me to understand more clearly? Will you help me to believe that I did not spend the winter alone? Will you help me not to rush through the important things? Will you help me to be able and willing? Will you help me find joy and then keep it? Will you save some treasures in a wooden box, and then will you take them out to show me sometimes? Will you love and not forget? Will you keep your spark?

It will be hard, it will all be hard.

Fifteen

I imagine you standing at the top of a high diving
board and what lies beneath you, instead of a blue pool,
is this world.

Your father is at the doctor again, and I realize the
thing he is most afraid of is that there will be no find-
ings from all the tests he has ordered, and he will be
told, simply, *We still don't know.*

"And what will you do if they tell you that?"

"I'll tell them I'm not leaving 'til they come up
with something."

Walking home, I took a different route. I couldn't tell you why until I stopped beneath the evergreen and listened. A hundred soft sounds I didn't understand until I realized it was the pine cones snapping open in the sun.

That night, I took your father there. We stood under the tree in the dark with our faces lifted and hoped that the branch we were under would be the next to sound.

I am building a house brick by brick. I don't even know what it looks like, just that I am handed a brick, which I place, and then I wait for another.

We went back to the arboretum, to see the eagles, but the eagles were elsewhere. Everything was blooming pink or white and the people there were happy— happy to be there, simply receiving.

"Look," your father said, "even the shadows are purple."

Later, much later, we will speak about the sky, how it held us, what it meant—that we were now both bigger and smaller than we had thought.

Your father is anticipating a parts swap—pieces of motorcycles laid out on tables for trade or for sale.

"How do you know they will have the part you need?" I asked.

"You don't."

I brought your father to the beach. I picked him up in his own car and took the corners fast. Even though it was only April, there were people on the margin of sand, between one kind of dark and another, with bonfires going.

Your father did not want to get out of the car.

"Come on," I said, "let's see the seals."

We could hear them, barking, not far off. But we could not see them after all—they were out in the waves of the Sound and their black matched the water's.

"At least there are mountains," your father said.

"Yes, at least there are."

And we left.

There is a tree full of birds this morning, little ones, quick-talking, and I look at them and think: They will choose the strong and sound partners for their mates, the healthy ones, the ones who can fight.

This morning, your father stared at his back in the mirror.

"What are you doing?" I asked.

"Trying to see the pain."

At the point when it is hard enough, too hard to bear, we like to believe that we will break through into a new place, a different place, one which will be easier than the last for all the work we have put into getting there.

It occurs to me that sometimes, the difficulty is unrelenting, and we do not get the story we wanted— the story of perseverance through long odds.

Each crow has chosen for itself a mate and a pine tree and is now constructing a nest stick by stick.

This year, when I see their grey-eyed fledglings, unable to fly, I will not rescue them and take them home in a box. I will know this is just a part of their learning.

We all have those stories which are bigger than we are, and which we must deliver accurately, free from our own ornamentation, because they are vast and hardly ours.

Your father spent the night in the garage, taking a

motorcycle to pieces so he could get at the heart of the matter. And when he had, and had installed a new part, and fit it all back together, the battery still did not charge.

He was half-asleep, but I asked anyway, "Will you ever get rid of that motorcycle?"

"No."

"Good. It's nice to have something to keep."

Now, there is a place on the sidewalk where the blackberry bush has taken over, and a path across the grass that shows that people do not fight it.

Your father's ankle is all blue—blue where he fell riding in the woods, and blue where the machine he was riding fell, too.

"Every time you ride off on your motorcycle, I say a prayer," I tell him, rubbing a salve on the wound.

"To who?" he asks. "To God? To an omniscient narrator?"

Easter. Down by the lake, a man is waxing the bottom of a needle-shaped boat with a gesture that looks like love.

"Every year," your father says, "I watch the tree outside my window open into buds, and the buds into little balls, and the balls into leaves. But today, I looked outside to see that the leaves were already there, completely open. And I said to the tree, *What? You didn't wait for me?*"

On my birthday, the sun at the kitchen table is a sure and sudden force. I eat my breakfast blinded and then there is a shadow and a crow sitting on the closest branch, not watching us, but present. As though he has been called.

"It's our crow," your father says, and it is an easy thought. I have just had it, too. We all want to believe in sudden blessings.

We had been in the museum. The exhibit had been a series of heavy mobiles made of steel, and I went through blowing on them carefully when the guards were turned away.

"They are nothing without their movement," I said, and your father blew on them too, but they stood still. "Look," I said, "there is one place on each that acts like a sail, and the trick is to find it."

After all the crying and all the conversation comes a moment on the couch where I look at your father and say, "When I see the whole of your life—the things you have wanted, worked for, kept—and take it against the whole of mine, it becomes clear. We don't want the same things. I want people and connections, and you want to be going somewhere fast and out of sight."

"But it sounds so nice," he says, "a family, a home."

"Nice," I say, "but not so nice that you will change things for it."

They have awarded her a prize, this author, for the book she wrote about the suicide of her husband.

A breathtaking achievement, they say.

Your father is about to walk out the door.

"Look," I tell him, "what do you do with your love? Where do you keep it? There are so many things you could do right now to show me that you care, but you've opted for none of them. Not a single one."

He sits in the chair in the hall and ties his shoes. Winds the excess lace around the ankles.

I pull him to his feet. "Look," I say, "the people you love, you must tell them all the time. You have to let them in. You have to be touched by them."

Of course, he has to do nothing just because I have said so.

"My umbrella is completely broken," said S. "I may need to share yours."

I look at it. Somehow, every single point has fallen from every single rib, but the whole thing is still reparable.

Your father lies on the couch and cries, and his tears form a wet exclamation point on the pillow.

"Some time," I say, "some time, can you tell me what you think about this all?"

He shakes his head.

"No?" I ask.

He shakes his head again, "I can't."

"That's been the problem all along."

There is a sound I do not recognize—a soft scraping. I cannot tell how far it is or where it is coming from.

"What is that?"

"The tree. Scratching the window by your desk."

"Does it want to come in?"

"No. It wants to communicate."

Your father does not dream, or he does not remember his dreams. When I ask him, in the café, whether he had any dreams last night, I did not expect a yes.

"I was on a boat, inside, and through the glass I could see people on a deck—laughing, talking, having fun. I wanted to be with them out there, but I couldn't get out. I picked up a chair and held it up to break through, but then...I woke."

"What do you think about that?"

"Nothing. It was just a dream."

Sixteen

Long ago, a story was written for me, and it was whole and long and, in parts, quite beautiful.

I took it in my hands and it was not long before the impact of the world had shattered that story into a thousand little shards. Some hardly big enough to see myself in.

Your father emerges, warm from the bed, and I catch him on his way to the bathroom. "Come here," I say, and I hold him in a hug that he neither resists nor helps to create.

The map on the wall behind him, the Yukon, the

word UNEXPLORED written across it expansively. And then: *Supposed course of Macmillan River.*

Imagine, I think bitterly, *that they discovered there is nothing there—no river, no land, nothing at all. That the map-makers were mistaken. Here, one simply drops off the face of the earth.*

They tore the building down before beginning the new one. Your father was right—for a while, the view was improved.

There is a bar by the airport where we will go if we are trying to test our luck, or if we are early. We order two drinks and something greasy, and I look out the window at the access road and the traffic and an improbable Japanese maple tree.

"I want to write something else."

"And stop the book?"

"I don't know."

"But it's the most exciting part. Will we break up?" There is a small smile ready to appear on his face.

"It's already so far from the book I wanted to write," I say, and I realize that what I actually want is to set my life down for a while.

A disc arrived in the mail with a note from my father. Three and a half minutes of footage from the pond. I am a child.

Your father watches it in tears and tells me, "You still swim like that. On your back and splashing everywhere."

It is a mixture of fear and determination. Navigating through an element where I am not at home.

"For next class," she had said, "please bring in a book you can destroy. We'll take it apart to see how it is made."

A picture in which the door between us became a character.

A picture in which the loved one did not leave.

A picture in which green predominated.

A picture in which I used all that was available to me.

I asked for something serious, but nothing came. I asked for information, for perspective, for a timeline, a length of rope, a fact to walk towards, but nothing came.

I had to make this, inch by inch, into what it is

today, as in the dark as anyone.

I did a handstand against the closet door on my birthday. My thirty-second birthday and the skirt of my dress fell over my eyes, and I remembered, inside the tent of my garment, the joy that is still mine, just a piece of it.

How it will be when, one day, I take this book off the shelf and read it. I will say, *Oh yes. That was the year when I lost you and then the years when your father and I lost each other. And I was even lost to myself for a while because there was an outcome I wanted, and I was so attached to it.*

I have taken your father's car south to the airport and the moon is either about to be full or just was. It is one of those late spring evenings tipping into blue and even the stilts supporting the runway lights over the highway create a beautiful and lonely architecture. The cottonwood is blowing its seed straight at me— soft in the gathering night.

I think about the difference between what we imagine and what we have actually made of this world and I think, *Keep me here. Keep this car and this night ever coming. Let me be always on my way to the*

airport, always on my way to a reunion, caught in an anticip-
ation that never ends.

"I love you," he said, and the words fell out of him like a current, like a quantity of water.

A man was standing on the street corner shouting, "God, why are you doing this to me? Don't you want me to want anything?"

The particular mystery of the teapot trick, where the audience can call out any beverage—soda water, hot tea, pink lemonade—which the pot will then produce.

Of course, I want to know how it is done, but I also want to preserve the delight.

I was touched that morning—touched by something. The quietness of the day arriving; the way, above the sounds of the bus turning the corner, there was bird song. The cars would soon be arriving at the little school, the children shouting greetings to each other from the edges of the intersection, where they stood with their parents and waited to cross.

That was it—I was able to single out one day from the long line of them, tirelessly repeating, and find it brightly unique. Its own.

Your father and I find a place in the arboretum where it would be easy to imagine you are in an actual forest except for the identification placard reading TRUE ASHES, and the clear, wide footpath behind us. There is a huge and tangled beauty-bush whose branches bow to make a cave large enough to stand in.

"I'll live here," I say. "You can bring me sandwiches and when you stay the night, we can look out through the branches at the stars."

There is a heron I see now, all the time, flapping from east to west or from west to east with great seriousness. It is morning or it is late in the day or it is any odd hour at all and I watch out of whichever window is nearest to find him there, like a secret that was never mine to keep.

I wanted a child I could speak to about plants. To whom I could explain the fact that plants choose to stay where they are and let things come to them.

"Throw it away," your father says. "It isn't even white anymore."

The fabric is foxed, old, and the wear, it shows.

"But I wore it that summer."

In the fields, under the sun, with dust all around, there is a picture of me in this dress and my face still bears a trace of my child face. That trace is gone now. I am too old for this dress. I throw it away.

"You aren't staying with yourself," she says. "It isn't about him. It's clearly not about him. Stay with you. What is this story actually about?"

It is actually about fear. Not a single fear, but a dense wall of smaller ones—each of which I have handled and placed with care. I can look at them. I can name them.

In that instant, I am filled with shame.

I am afraid your father will never be well.

I am afraid I am dulling myself.

I am afraid he will never allow himself to be known.

I am afraid of a hungry heart.

I am afraid there is not enough passion.

Shall I continue.

I confess to having wanted answers.

I admit I had believed, and parts of me still do, that

it was possible to approach the coming chapters of my life with certainty, rather than stepping out blindly and seeing if the ledge would hold.

He is sick more often than he is well.

"We live across from the warehouse where they build props for the ballet," I tell her. The counselor. The one who shows us to ourselves. "A hulking expanse of grey building that seems heavy and ordinary. Every once in a while, they'll work with the doors open. There are worlds inside—forests and Greek columns and rose trellises. And your thoughts about the building change because you know now all that is inside of it."

There is a pause.

"That's him—that's who he is. I live for the moments when he opens the doors."

A small child stops me on the way home.

"Excuse me," she says, "do you go to the moon?"

"No," I tell her. "Why do you ask?"

"Your helmet…"

"This? This is for a motorcycle," I explain.

When seen from a great enough distance, anything

becomes wonderful—a silo, an alley, a neighborhood. The blight is hidden and the pattern is revealed.

We were falling asleep when your father asked me to explain it to him—the lyrebird. "I'm not sure I understand," he said, "how the lyrebird is significant."

I found my phone in the dark and played him the video—the lyrebird in the forest singing the sounds of the kookaburra, the chainsaw, the camera shutter. I played him the video of the lyrebird in the zoo singing the sounds of large animals, and a hammer on an empty structure, and then one person's voice at one moment in time—*What are you doing?*

"Isn't it incredible?" I say.

He agrees.

"The sounds," he says, "are so true to life."

"I guess I am trying," I continue, "to capture my world in a similar way. To get close to all of it. To hold the moments since this conversation began. To play them back to someone I love."

"It makes sense," he says, and turns to sleep.

So I lie in the dark and think of the lyrebird and realize he does what he does much better than I will ever do because there are no sections of the song that he prefers, no pieces not beautiful enough to include.

Even the destruction. He sings it all.

Notes

p. 3   David Attenborough, BBC Wildlife
        – youtu.be/VjE0Kdfos4Y

p. 25   text taken from an exhibit at the Museum of
        Jurassic Technology, re. Nicola Sabbatini

p. 61   sign text taken from *Masnavi* by Rumi
        [transl. Edward Henry Whinfield (1898)]

p. 66   lyrics from 'Rumor of Mormons' by Robin
        Holcomb (song cycle: *We Are All Failing Them*)

p. 75   interpretations by Ginger Schenck
        – lenormandquest.blogspot.com

p. 113 Professor Andrei Linde, Stanford University
        – youtu.be/ZlfIVEy_YOA

p. 133 Chook at Adelaide Zoo, Zoos SA
        – youtu.be/WeQjkQpeJwY

Acknowledgements

My deepest thanks to *Black Warrior Review*, in whose pages a portion of this book first appeared, and to Jenny Boully, for her support of this work in its early stages. Gratitude to the Vermont Studio Center, for time and space in the snowy season, to Becca Johnson Grozinsky for her faith and enthusiasm, and to Mary Hoyt for always knowing. Thank you to Amelia Riedler for waiting to hold this book in her hands, and to Jacqueline Suskin for keeping the flame lit. And thank you to Marisa Vitiello, Tom Yoder, Melanie Noel, and Shin Yu Pai, for friendship, affirmation, and creative community. Gratitude to David, without whom there would be neither bird nor book.

Thanks also to Michelle Tudor and Peter Barnfather, for clarity of vision, and for giving these words such a beautiful home.

Meredith Clark is a poet and writer whose work has received *Black Warrior Review*'s nonfiction prize, and appeared in *Phoebe*, *Gigantic Sequins*, *Denver Quarterly*, *Berkeley Poetry Review*, *Poetry Northwest*, and elsewhere. She lives in Seattle, and is currently at work on a second book.